My
First Trip
To The
Dentist

Carolyn N Paulino
Illustrated by: Sierra Mon Ann Vidal

THE ERIC HOFFER AWARD
FINALIST
Excellence in Independent Publishing

Print information available on the last page

Rev. date: 04/24/2017

To order additional copies of this book, contact:
Xlibris
1-888-795-4274
www.Xlibris.com
Orders@Xlibris.com

You are fearfully and wonderfully made

Psalm 139:14

Today I took my first trip to the dentist! It was so exciting!

When we arrived at the dentist's office, I got to play in a play area while we waited patiently for my name to be called.

"Luis!" called the very nice lady in uniform. It was finally my turn!

The lady in uniform took me in a room where I got to meet the dentist and even took a ride on a really cool chair!

9

Wow! That was fun!

"See these? This is a tooth counter and a tooth mirror. With these, I'll count your teeth and I'll make sure you are sugar-bug free."

"Open big like an alligator," said the dentist, and she started saying the *ABC*s to count my teeth.

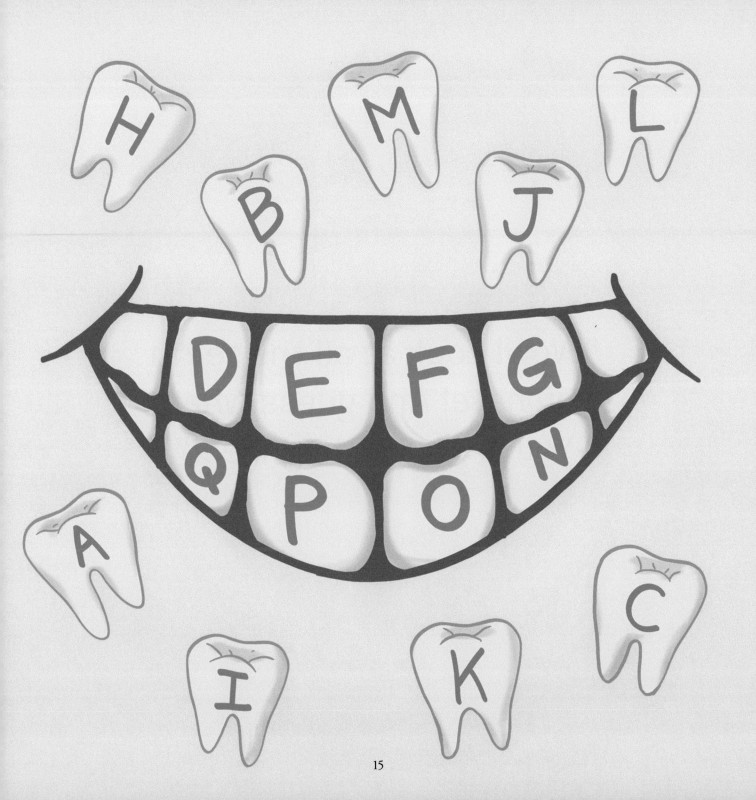

"Wow! Look at all the teeth you have! And guess what! You are sugar bug-free!"

And just like that, we were all done! Going to the dentist was so much fun! I even got a goodie bag to take home.

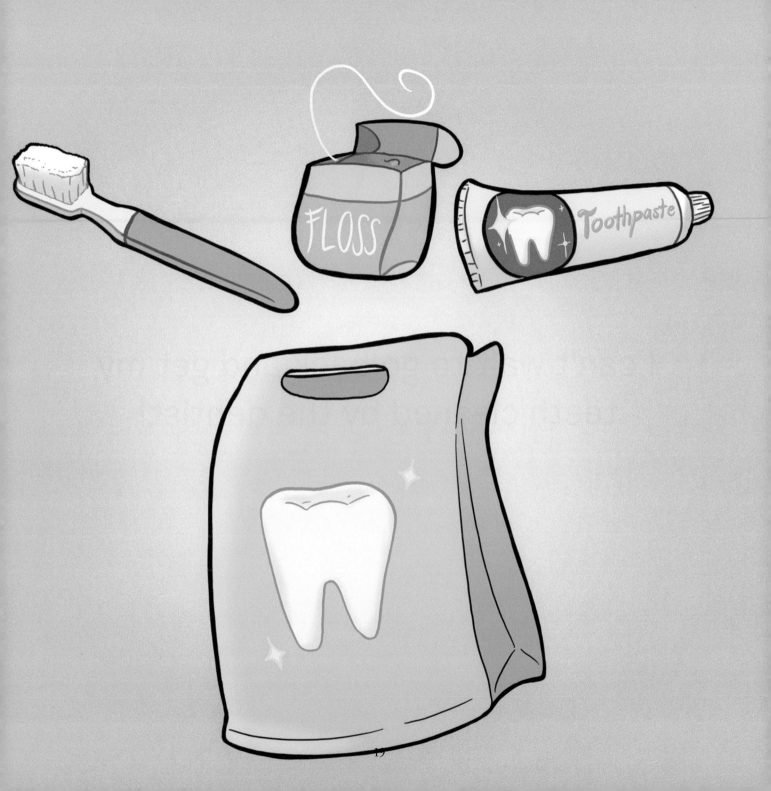

I can't wait to go back and get my teeth cleaned by the dentist!

Printed in the United States
By Bookmasters